Solar Winds

by

Marc J. LaFountain

DANCING CROWS
PRESS

ISBN 13: 978-1-951543-14-3

The cover art is a 2014 watercolor by the author entitled "Origin….Unknown".

Cover design by Colin Wheeler, MFA, ABD
Strickenbrow.com or strickenbrow@gmail.com

My deep gratitude to Elyse Wheeler for her careful editing, formatting and production of this book.

Dedication

For Phil Mengel, 1950-2016
you will always radiate

Butterfly

I put my face where
a yellow swallowtail lights,
it too a flower
in that verdant bush amidst
those delicious dusty colors
on its delicate, weightless body
lilting on its antelope ballerina legs.

You cannot touch a butterfly,

that's beyond possible,
beyond touch, where your
otherwise nimble, dexterous fingers
are blunt and dumb,
insensitive,
useless.

You can touch them only
when your eyes have wings
that let you land silent as
dust on down,

touch them only when
your own fluttering body's
mysterious colors
hover in the air,
subtly entangled,
already mingled with theirs

before you ever knew
those colors that light
on a flower
on a shrub,
on a face.

Oh no, unless you know how
you cannot touch a butterfly.

Gazing is an Art

How boring we thought,
the old men sitting on their porches,
seemingly vacant,
sitting in silence,
whittling the while,

staring into space,

whittling away all that is
superficial, inconsequential.

But then we never smelled the rain,
saw the lightning in their eyes

never knew they pondered
the dragonfly's flight,
the strange alchemy of leaves
turning yellow to gold

never knew how they speculated
on why the black gum makes
vivid red leaves midsummer when
all else is vibrant green.

a red leaf? an omen?

We never knew the strange
exotic botanicals in their
favorite gins and bitters that
so enchanted them,

never knew they wondered
what, in the emergent spring, will surprise them,
and what will not,
if they will ever see again
the hummingbirds' return,
the ephemeral perennials' annual flush,
their vivid reds, opaque whites,
the cacophony of the spring frogs.

We never knew they had dug
several feet straight down
in the red clay and had
seen the ashes of ancient fires,
covered now with the newer ashes of
beloved friends,
the cats and dogs they grieved.

Never knew they were pilgrims
who knew the fearless are not just those
looking forward to unknown futures,
but those too who ply the stuff
of days already gone,
their deep forests and crevasses,
their pitfalls and exultations.

We never knew the shavings they
whittled away became their ashes,
scattered in the days
that burned around them.

On the inadequacy of prepositions

Listening to the weatherman tell of a front
moving on off over into
a nearby county,
she changed out her oversized sunglasses,
put down her box of Cheezits,
threw back her hair,
popped her bubblegum,
and commenced to sippin' on a soda -
a Southern girl sippin' on a soda.

Sippin' on?

On?

How do you sip ON something?

Maybe sip up?
Or just plain sip?
Surely though never sip into or around
and, heavens, not beyond.

Prepositions: connective tissues,
tenuous directional adhesives,
tangential, superficial,

and though intimate,
forever proximate,

about the best that can
be done when all you have
is a straw.

when

when i was younger
i moved in the shadows of entropy
secure from, oblivious to
its embrace

now inevitability
is ever more certain
forcing amendments to
my sense of immortality

before long the morning sun
will come through the
east window
without me as witness,

i will have already left
to become
the one who left behind
the stone walls,
the ephemerals by the creek,
the paths in the woods and meadows,
anonymous rocks on trails no one will ever see,
crystals by the little pond.

Anaphylaxis

Ana
Ana Phylaxis
she no friend of mine
you don't even want to know her

uninvited, but lurking round the corner,
she came calling one day
sneaking on the wings of wasps
to take my love away

under Ana's spell I watched her
collapse unconscious at the edge of
the end of days

Ana - she no friend of mine
she no prophet
no subtle seductress
you don't even want to know her

only by chance or grace I there then
when she burst in

trembling in panicked horror
I pierced my love with a magic pen
to countermand that wicked
venomous needle the witch had used
to steal my love,

bringing her to life
to rise again,
one more chance to breathe

Ana - you no friend of mine,
and you,
you don't ever want to know her

A Spot of Bother

snake bit and all stove up,
he was always a day late
and shorter than before,

misfiring even when firing
before aiming,
he damaged goods.

mistakenly seen a feckless liar
or pitiful fool,
he was just way over all the lines
visible too late only from their traverse,
unwittingly reckless
his only luck bad
his only fortune missed
destiny deferred.

unfolding beyond the pale,
deprived of the counsel of Tralfamadore,
he was a pilgrim unstuck in time
but stuck in the craw of life
fated never to be a pearl

the only break he ever got
was a breach of continuity,
he, a master of accidental non sequiturs,
unable even to go in circles,
which might have comforted him immensely,
an ouroboros who didn't know his
arse from his mouth
or any other hole in space into which,
inevitably, he would stumble.

born again

St Vitus ain't got nothin' on 'em now
they've sipped salvation cocktails
strychnine sometimes lye
streaming in their veins
they're dancing in the stars

trance dancing with serpents,
the copperheads and rattlers
trancing too yet ready to take
those reeking of fear - the mark of the
unfaithful and the unforgiven -
or just those whose time had come

even the clumsy nimble in their rapture
skipping feverishly in crooked symmetry
whirling dervishes wrestling fire
they're all eat up with charisma

holy rolling in the numinous deep
their speaking tongues vipers
in their skulls casting out demons
and sorcerers that they dread

hands in the air like Simon says
waving around like they just don't care
ecstatic elsewhere eyes ready for
divine visitations of grace
a holy ghost descending

laying hands on their
wretched bodies and sorry
tattered souls rising them up
delivering them the promise
their faith alone reveals

slain in the spirit
losing their balance
falling down writhing
paralyzed and still
lost but never lost
in the glory of their lord

Inspiration

after the breath of fire,
Newton had a urethra moment when
the splendid apple of wisdom
tumbled out of the ethereal fallopian
hidden in the sky that had just
rippled when Jack shook the thigh
bone and the hip bone to which
it was connected

sending that celestial red orb
streaking across the planes of
the familiar and the unacknowledged,
feathering them with ley lines
that fooled sages into believing
their truths, from which we
now untangle ourselves

it

it is not the incessant murmuring
it is the it that murmurs
the it that murmurs
murmurs

so, here for you is a diversion
offered as a moment
of relief from the
odious regime of
the same

and from the murmuring
that cannot be still in the night
when all a body wants is silent slumber

here then an escape
a space of delight

a poet's imaginary magic

it too though fraught
with clues that ensnare
your imagination,
vex your time,
stripping them of their
safety in endless repetition,
plunging them otherwise
into the rippling echoes
of yet another unfathomable
font of enigmas
where they revel freely

throwing anchors
into the wind
to watch them
and wonder

I i

I: quirk and device
of a language that makes
of me a one letter word,
capitalized,
or not

I: always first, exceptional
the obstinate hubris of a script of
singularity, insularity,
capitalized, subjecting all
to swirl in its orbit.

but i am not that I,
and, not always insisting on that ploy,
i oft decapitate that I,
becoming a lower case
that comports with what surrounds,
whose aesthetics do not assert
the sovereignty of formality's
correctness and conventions
informing the swirls of its orbit

i can be taller than a
tree or mountain
without being I

Radiolarians

snowflakes in the sea,
hot air balloons floating in
the underwater sky,
their glorious skeletons ablaze
in shapes imaginations could not fathom

a flotilla of spires and angles,
their edges sharp, soft, rococo,
arched and gothic,
splendid, slender spirals
kaleidoscopic colors radiating
from their tiny ivory shells

quartz and mineral,
delicate, ornate,
outrageous but never ostentatious,
living protean scaffolds made solid by
the draft of some ingenious architect

elegant mandalas
never at a loss for symmetry

Saving a life

one chilling night before time,
I saw through prussian blue light
the hole in the dark gray mountain
into which the one I could never love would disappear
instantly, silently, forever

but that dream was nothing next to when,
by chance, I fumblingly wrenched you from
the abyss into which you had been pushed

such things are possible
when time has not yet arrived

Solar Winds

Chasing the magic nymphs
of fata morgana, I ate
the flesh of the gods,

became channeled blood
streaming protozoan rays
flowing out, away,
lightspeed along a cosmic pole
stretched out in empty endless space,

my soul besieged, flagging in
those solar winds.

Beyond all boundaries,
dancing with demise,
hanging on for life,
all I am, or was, gone.

Could not have known better,
no avatar am I,

the folly of my courage bared,
my false idolatry
mocked now by
those torrential gales,

for knowing letting go
would be,
will be,
permanent,
forever.

Cringing, I beseeched
those gods:
rescind the winds!
silence all sirens!
take down this humbled flag from
that forsaken pole on whose void
it flaps in flogging solar winds.

Something between bodies

ties them together
when in each other's presence

something about bodies
beckons and tunes in
like radar rhyming cellos

like the tremors that shudder me
when I see

the mangled body of the
opossum on the road
its head grotesquely turned,
a horrifying shape to its mouth,
perhaps from some final primal
howl or scream

the whales trapped in arctic ice
with one small hole
from which to draw air where
what is most palpable is the
sound of their gasping breaths

the cashier's head stiffly cocked askew,
her withered arm working with the unaffected one
to move groceries along the
conveyor belt ever so deliberately,
ever so gracefully

theirs is not my struggle
but it is

something there arrests and summons my body
long before I know it has,
forcing it to linger with them,
not in pity or compassion, but
according to some circuitry
where we are invisible sides
of each other's visibility.

Dad's ashes

it is no ignominious turn that
for his ashes I have no urn

keeping them instead in a small
clear jar, formerly the place of
homemade jam, where I see them without
worrying they'll be spoiled by light,
amazed they show no signs of entropy

no fancy bowl or vase for them,
the bulk, and the bulk of the ashes
of a loved one are indeed heavy,
buried next to my mother,
in the earth,
the remainder here with me

I sprinkle them out by the swing
near the pond where he and my little
white dog sat in the shade of a battered,
tough old pine

scatter them on the deck where
he once told me,
in Alzheimerian verse,
he thought the dead flowers
in the dry pots were beautiful

what had I missed?

before I left the house
built with my bare hands
I scattered one last pinch
in the room where he slept
when visiting

where the rest will rest
is yet untold
but one day it will be
my turn to burn
I hope for me there'll be no urn

prayers without words

sometimes they are guttural, visceral,
searingly wrenching,
other times softly transcendent

they might begin whole
other times stuttering fragments, spasms,
mysteries often clear as
icicles in silver skies

they can be incandescent
scorching all with their light.
other times subtly liminal
hovering in some strangely familiar space.

some arrive on wings, unprovoked,
announcing themselves gratuitously,
according to their own whim and time,
harbingers of words never to be thought or spoken.

not always for some avatar, god or religion,
they send souls skittering,
like flat stones thrown by a child across still water,
oft their only destiny to crash
on some cliff or shore.

they are mercury,
slippery, elusive
like a bead of water
on a waxy leaf

sometimes a screeching, wailing plea
other times the colored arias of
songbirds and blue dragonflies

what?

me?

pray?

dreaming of a storm

lying sleeping dreaming storming
clouding whiting lightning flashing
in the very ceilings of my brain
awaking blacking bursting crashing
funnels twisting fears immense

stretching out in all directions for returning answers
but no hiding shelters are there from cascading
voices coming in on strands of open void
that awe to silence ready i will go

Radiate

Time   Float   Fade   Radiate

Time is a phantasy,
an illusion.

But sometimes time
is handy to have around -
you can do things with it.

Still, an illusion.

Having crossed where shamans go,
he knew that too.

And he knew the myth of gravity.
When everything else was following it down,
he said he would not go into that night.

Rather, he would float.
He would float in the skies
on the winds.

Soon orange and yellow leaves were tumbling
to the place whose only promises are
dust and silence.

He was in slow motion then.
The pace of the arc of his fork,
ascending from his plate to his mouth,
languished in empty space.

The sumac was red,
the bald cypress somewhere
between green and sienna.
Faint then, he turned his head to look
but his eyes lingered behind,
arriving later.

Maybe dreaming,
he lost his thoughts in
the quickening of the stilling.

Yet always, with grace, he leaned forward
into his future knowing that
this dimming is irrelevant.

Out on his beloved pond,
with the water that floated his raft
spilling out of his eyes,
he tearfully told me one day:
If I cannot float,
I do not want to live.

Later on he said he would simply do
what the blonde singer told us once:
fade away and radiate.

That's what he said he would do:
fade away and radiate.
There would be no more
white-coated witch doctors,
no knives, no treacherous machines.

In the days after I told him all the things
you'd tell someone you love
before those chances slip away.

When the days and breaths grew sparse
I drew him close and whispered:
you might fade away,
but you will always radiate,
always radiate.

A metal ghost now dwells the field
where once - for sale - his tractor sat.

It was cold then,
the late afternoon winter sun golden
on the barks of the woods,
chilling even more knowing
he had left us to ourselves.

Yet always there is the warm
he radiates.
Yes, my floating friend,
you will always radiate,
always radiate.

Alexander's poet

we were avid and aflame
but there was no rapture
no happy ending
that night we celebrated
his tragic ravaged life
draped in the silken violence
of your rending lines each syllable and
word threaded together lovely
as he himself might have fashioned

bringing life to him again
the wonder that he was
bright again in the costumes
in the swagger
in the inflections of the models
who braved the cold that night
nothing compared to the numb
that must have been his body
when he decided irretrievably
he was done

woven too in those racking words
were filaments of your own introverted anguish
loss of family and love
wrong turns undeserved by a gentle soul
shreds of pain protruding raw
unadorned by blush or guise
honest there for all to hold

in the white room we felt
each other's wincing sighs
a rippling lament recoiling
from body blows delivered by
those visceral verses

souls touched by his
and by his poet,
we took the weight home
with us that night and
released it to the sky

heard them drums

we were all in the
pool that day when
we floated him on
our memories like
seals bouncing a ball
with their noses in
the sky

which is where they
knew he went
or maybe to the sea
that bore the seals themselves)

floated him like he
the big drummer boy
floated those sticks
on his beloved drums

we heard them drums
and gave him life again
or he us
for maybe it was he
who conjured us
to move to sounds
we knew him for

all he wanted was to bang on
the drums all day
and before he left he did

all he wanted besides
floating on a raft in his pond
on a day when we were
all in the pool together

that big pool we all dwell
til that day we become
those balls of memories

At the old Polish church

On a frigid Wisconsin Christmas Eve
there were diamonds everywhere

the road we took there a tunnel
without a roof, the snow
a telephone pole high
touching the wires that
strung together a forest of sticks
in the silent night,
in the utterly vivid white
of the snow where
there were crystals everywhere.

Way below zero
I feared my face would freeze.
Ablaze in ambient candleglow
the warmth of the dimly lit gingerbread church
shone everywhere through flaming crystals,
tiny prisms falling from the sky

At four generations my family
was still young,
for all around us there were elders,
like diamonds they were everywhere.

An old world Polish spirit
echoing some primal gathering
from whence they came,
and oh those joyful carols on which they returned
to those places with tears in their eyes.

Old women in long, plain, dark coats,
babushkas covering their heads while
they were in the house of the master,
the old men reverent but daydreaming
of a heaven with those diamonds everywhere,
and squirming children, I among them,
trying to touch their light.

Solstice

Mysterious and strange how we are so
captivated by the arrival of the time of
utter darkness and the numinous black,
some fascinated, some in dread,
perhaps because it aligns with the opaque
and occluded accompanying
each of us at every turn

We seek, even conjure that darkness,
not to anticipate light,
but to revel in the dark itself.

Oft we feign fear of the dark,
possible only if we are not tormented,
only if darkness is not too rampantly deep.

Darkness gone too far terrifies,
yet dark is not to be feared
but rather what emerges in the light,
light gone too far terrifies, too

For an old man solstices are
luminous pearls strung together
tracing a path called destiny,
relived in circles in the sky.

In the Living Room, After Christmas

Eyes are everywhere,
year after year after year,
but rarely if ever is there eye to eye,
except in fantasy or memory

Eyes are everywhere,
alive once again in the afterglow
of the advent and withdrawal of Christmas,
in the anticlimactic backwash that travels on
waves of sentimentality and nostalgia

Faced by eyes everywhere:

Trimmed with worried, warning brows,
the dark, intense orbs of the taught,
vigilant nutcracker forever poised
to crack a nut.

Flanked by him another,
this one with a beehive and a bee proof veil:
a nutcracker with bees?

The eyes of black and white Scotties in
a red reed basket,
those of a fawn in alert, wary wonderment,
devoid of fear or bewilderment.

The eyes of reindeer, snowmen, kittens
those of owls, rabbits, mice and peacocks,
and those of countless versions
of the jolly red shaman

They anoint the tree of honor,
its decorated greenery set alight
to celebrate in the dark light of solstice time,

There are eyes of mermaids, seahorses, cherubs,
especially those bright eyes of children,
their delicate innocence suspended forever
In ornaments cherished by their parents.

Marked by things known only to those
who placed them there,
always the phantom eyes of family
and other loved beings long departed,

Eyes call us out,
away from our interior circuitry,
summoning us to pass through and abandon
what we have built around ourselves,
to venture into the dark in search of light,
into the light to find the dark

The Great Beauty

is a tangled, restive muse,
an alluring stream we hope,
in defiance of the tao,
to step in twice, or more,

but it is given only in specks
and riotous outbursts, according
to the age of the day and when
it is not secret or overly vain.

No minion of nostalgia,
the Great Beauty is a conspirator
reveling in the opulence of an opening
that oft distracts those mired in melancholy
who cannot fathom the days of passed futures.

The Great Beauty is a fool's diamond,
amuse bouche for a tattered soul,
a blank and black comedy rendered
colorful sentimentality by a charlatan's
wistful lament,

a street of crocodiles you will never cease to roam,
where time appears to have arrived
but slips about, or has been deferred,
or has already slithered by,
perishing, taking with it
the uncoordinated pieces you
thought were your enduring substance.

Yet it too is an oddity in a precious clearing,
sometimes everywhere,
charmingly blooming underfoot,
even now,
in utter decadence.

When I wrote

I was the ghost of Artaud's hand,
graphite digits, dark,
figuring the cruel,
intending fluidity in
movements otherwise jerky and halting,
taunting and enticing the reader

but really only harrowing the space
where writing contorts,
turns on itself,
becoming acrobatic and ridiculous:

pathetically necessary,
wickedly unavoidable.

Oh the cruelty of
disappearance hitched to
words that slip toward and by
what they seek but cannot
convene or coalesce.

There in the silent commotion
of those words lies the ruination
of the writer, the disaster
whose body writes and writhes,
draws and curls in tormented, scribbling joy,
a body that cannot be but disfigured

for when it is not so marred
and no longer twists,
it has died
an even more cruel death
than when writing,
when persisting in a life
without phantom beauty.

Cataract

tannic yellow tints
the rims where light enters,
beckoning and foretelling of
the dimming,

that space where the light of
dissipation travels.

hazy ochre washes shade
theaters where colored events
and things once conspired
in utter visibility.

what is seen when not seeing happens
is seeing what one is not supposed to see,
hopes not to see -
the procession of the dimming.

what is seen when
not seeing happens
is entirely something else:

the wending paths where
the many but numbered
ends of days abscond
in sepia and sienna

Numan's Aura

wrapped in shadowy, ambient gray
altered only by a diffuse white
hovering low like ground fog or
some mysterious vapor,
the empty stage once flat
now tiered away from the audience,
the farthest rows back the highest
mountains over clouds

bathed in blue green light
the clear acrylic drums and organs
shone in luminous transparency,

in white suits,
carbon black hair,
lavish red lip gloss,
the musicians appeared
on a clear invisible stage

aural bodies becoming solid,
suspended, floating in the rays
and waves of rhythms they summoned
from some unknown place
we all knew so well

the driveway

the uneven old brick road is
wavy and lumpy,
according to some discrepant,
if not decrepit,
moss between its toes.

forces that be soon will set
cement in that space,
and though I grasp reasons why
I want them to die,

for something primal rises in me:
some force of nature
unpredictable, uncontrollable.

that new, solid, impermeable surface
will intrude into the living green
and surrounding handmade walls of stone
promising to control water
and time,

but something aboriginal rises in me,
something to protect
what is still wild,
some defiant force of nature,

something rises in me
against the taming and the pacifying,
some Sisyphusean fury insolent
though it knows all that rise up disappear.

like some curator of
things ephemeral,
some voyeur at
a play that makes no sense,
something rises in me,
something against extinction
pissing into the winds
of what will come to pass

Starfire Drive

I live on star fire,
near echo lake,
helical piers and dead men buried
in my yard pull steel cables holding
my house to the edge of the ravine
where all around is precarious and in peril,

not of their own accord but
rather due to the well intentioned
but fumbling hands of humans.

round the bend in the gorge
near the old architect's abode
an owl in bright daylight snatches a chipmunk
as a black widow scurries into a crack
in a musty dank wall
when light falls on its
sticky silken web

time and water have ravaged roots and rocks
and the cedar boards covered
in shadows and speckled light
are disappearing in moist air

Nesting

Just as the dog
circles round and round
to find just the right place
to lay down,

and the dying old maple
sheds its bark in
strips spiraling downward,
leaning, falling, but not yet fallen,

I too turn and rearrange
under the sheets and covers
to locate that spot
where bed and body merge,
where the edge between them
disappears in silent sleep.

I dig and furrow,
moving plants and trees,
rocks and stones,
things alive and dead,
to just those spaces where
shards of leaves and
twists of dried grass become
particles of the dirt and air
into which I will settle
one last time.

Surfers

like the nuns at ocean's edge
in the haze of the early morning sun,
surfers pray for waves

in curling glass tubes with
mist trailing off their crests
they dream of where the ride is
slippery liquid mercury like

those volatile little slants and
rays of light that
find their way down
glistening, glowing shafts
to rest on stones, shells,
and sand below

those molten images
how do they do that?

Visions on the Ward

Before his eyes he saw the battered forms
of humans sideways in life, wondering if he himself
was one, these others but
what he had conjured, or what some other had
contrived for him.

A lady hung panicked from the ceiling by her heels
with serpents coiled and swirling all around
the inferno below,
Dante himself taking refuge in the shadows,

A shriveled man at a Dr. Joyce Brother's
talk, counting the times her eyes blinked,
knowing them as signals to the aliens, from whom
he hid, invisible behind his sunglasses,

A woman gazing in a mirror
seeing not her reflection in its shine, but
something ever more horrible which receded
and remained unspoken.

A young painter so frightened by the dark shadow
running in tangled black forests of red rain
that he destroyed his work to liberate himself,
but he could not - experimental fear gone wrong

He saw at least two faces of Eve, one a truck stop
slut in lurid clothes,
the other a timid, fawning believer in
the power of men and the Almighty

And then the son of God, a moving crystal pyramid
descended from the speed of light,
who with his blood drew crosses on his walls,
frightening all as if he were demonic,
which to himself he surely was,
he, his own quicksand.

Passerby

Last night having spoken so softly the truth
a man said of him free spirit be he.
Shortly the colors of light did then fade
to witness an entry,
a man and a song,
but hence having come from the shadow's reverse,
he appeared so real could spirit he be?

He could I could see yet he spoke as man
of distance from world, of dream plighted plan.
He screamed, he cried, he soared to the moon,
he pounded the floor and his heart fluttered strong
He laughed, he loved, he danced like a fool.
Twas plain to be seen his garden he longed
but shadows had gone leaving traces in time
and holes in spaces where suns had once shined.

often a poet's best friend

claiming their autonomy
words sometimes flow unfettered
and you don't know
where they're going or
what they mean
when acorns are buried in rich earth
covered with leaves
never to be found again by
twitchy squirrels that put them there
despite their constant searching

sometimes words are
mercury or ether and they
rise and breathe
hang in the air and dance like vapor
going where they please
sailing nocturnal avenues on
the other side of dreams
where ghost orchids sing

their nascent flowing lines often
blooming shapeless refrains
meandering like nomads
looking for a momentary home
playfully adrift of the hope
of scheme or sense

their flux the possibility of riffs
that never form
freedom's babble
costing nothing but the time
it takes to let them wander
the faith to follow their journey
or just a blindness to that faith

word salad

wondered about what it could be
what could it mean
even worried about what it would be if it befell me
then for some time now cataclysm has distended and
has been imminent in its immanence
the deluge succeeding ruptured structurlusions
synergizes toward what is to be
while through the rainbows of the truth
adversity turbulates to calm as
disintegrated souls become shadows of the flux
red lotus fires in the sky
prismatic light reveals
eternity's vast vision
witness to pasts passed painfully
to energies detached but fused uncanny to the void
the matrix of humanity entwined in silver cylinders
spun delicately for the infinite progression of the arc
where the dance of living is in the moment
they say though all time is hung about in memories of
colors to be cascaded in the form of ever
even right now

Morning in a Labyrinth

7:30 and the procession to infinity's
eternal passages where vibrations intersect
gazing bodies sitting up from dreaming
in a sunlit house to see that silver light pass through
the crystals of a chance

perhaps always the truth unspoken
though sensed at dawn by mutual vision of clear
spaces where boysenberry purple lends its shade
to golden time within which travel souls to memories
of phantasies of glimpses of the solid forms entwined
in velvet nothing dancing joy and god

haitu

1
constipated speech
escapes through
seething teeth
landing on
my brain
sending me
Into orbit

2
pacing shrimp
dancing to
bagpipe spacemusic
voraciously inhaled
unlimited meatballs

3
home is
that place
you once
already entered
long ago
and not
where they
take you
when you
have to
go there

4
ensconced in
vague vegetation's
wriggling orbs
nostalgic crickets
earnestly pursue
redundant salads

5
succinctly fulvous
tree ducks
gleefully ride
mood elevators
astride those
silly balloons
toward hazy
distant stars

6
destiny is
what happens
when you
are in
the process
of becoming
what you
will have
become when
you no
longer are

7
        hai

quite unwittingly
hospital acquired
infections inflect
the human
awareness institute

        tu

to too
i say
only two
one more
than one

tao

10,000 things
or more

emanate from
singular nothing

the same
never same

forget form
embrace mystery

Marc J LaFountain, born in Massachusetts, grew up on the east end of Long Island. After receiving his PhD in Sociology from the University of Tennessee, he taught at several universities before joining the University of West Georgia in 1977. He retired from there in 2008. He is the author of Dali and Postmodernism: This is Not an Essence (SUNY Press, 1997). His book of poems, Left Wanting More, was published by Vabella Press in 2015. He currently lives in Atlanta.